FORTUNE-TELLING
BOOK FOR BRIDES

This book belongs to

_____

The gift of

_____

K. C. Jones
Illustrations by A. J. Garces

CHRONICLE BOOKS
SAN FRANCISCO

THE PROPOSAL

Congratulations, bride-to-be! Your engagement is the first official step toward a blissful marriage. And the manner in which the two of you became engaged speaks volumes about your future life together. Whether the proposal was a complete surprise or you knew it was coming, whether your beloved got down on one knee or swept you off your feet when he asked you, whether it happened at home or on a romantic evening out—these all hold the key to what lies ahead. Read on. . . .

HOW YOU GOT ENGAGED

HIDDEN RING

If your engagement ring was hidden in something (a champagne flute, a box of chocolates), your life together will be full of excitement. Expect many happy surprises in the years to come.

ON BENDED KNEE

If your husband-to-be got down on one knee and proposed, it is likely that you will be parents to three or more children.

ON VACATION

Your life together will include much time for leisure. It is possible that either you or your husband will have a career in academia.

ON A HOLIDAY

Your marriage will be marked by a deep and abiding passion for one another. Your lives will be busy—but remember to set aside time to be alone together.

ON YOUR BIRTHDAY

You will always be first and foremost in your true love's heart, and you will return his feeling with equal ardor.

IN FRONT OF FRIENDS OR FAMILY

As a couple, you will seek the company of others frequently, and will have a thriving social life.

IN PUBLIC

You will take big risks together. But don't worry—they will pay off.

IN A WRITTEN MESSAGE

If the proposal came tucked in a fortune cookie, carved in the sand on a beach, as a message in a bottle, or in some other written form, your life together will be an unconventional one, but you will always be happy. Hold fast to your convictions—do not be influenced by what others think.

IF YOU DID THE ASKING

You will be the outwardly dominant member of the marriage. You are a discerning judge of character and you surround yourself with only those who have the highest ideals. Luckily, your husband-to-be fits the bill!

WHERE YOU GOT ENGAGED

AT A RESTAURANT

The two of you have expensive and cultured tastes. Fortunately, you will have the means to afford the lifestyle you desire. If you became engaged at a restaurant you had been to before, you already have your wealth, or it will follow quickly after marriage; if the restaurant was new to you, your fortune will come with time.

AT HOME

Neither of you is exceedingly outgoing, but in smaller groups you can prove to be very entertaining and gregarious. You will be liked a great deal by friends and acquaintances, and you will be exceedingly affectionate with your children.

BY THE OCEAN

At one point you believed you might never marry. But getting engaged by the ocean (especially at sunset or sunrise) symbolizes the freedom and sense of self that you will retain in your future marriage. You're ready for this next step; embrace the possibilities with open arms.

NEAR WATER

If you became engaged by a river, lake, or waterfall, the two of you will meet a new couple in the first year of marriage who will forever change your lives for the better.

OVER WATER

If the proposal took place on a boat, you and your mate will find great pleasure in helping others together. If it happened on a pier or jetty, the two of you will take enjoyment in nature and the outdoors.

BY TREES

Trees are symbols of life and the soul. Becoming engaged under a tree symbolizes that you and your future husband will shelter each other all your lives, and serve as a grounding influence for each other. Becoming engaged under a fruit-bearing tree, or a tree with new buds, represents fertility in your marriage.

NEAR MOUNTAINS

Mountains are good omens. Becoming engaged on a mountaintop foretells a marriage in which the two of you will win fame and recognition. On the other hand, becoming engaged at the base of a mountain, or within view of mountains, means that you and your partner will gain strength from each other for all your lives.

IN THE AIR

An engagement in an airplane, a hot-air balloon, or other flying craft symbolizes the potential for you and your love to reach great heights. You are known for your optimism and good humor, while he is thorough and diligent. You're better together than apart—pool your strengths and you will be unstoppable.

ON STAIRS

Stairs represent decisiveness. Becoming engaged at the top of a set of stairs, or on an upper story of a building, points to the fact that the future marriage is exactly the right decision. A spiral staircase has much the same portent, but also augurs longevity for the couple. And an engagement on a balcony means that you and your love may spend long stretches of time apart during your marriage— but these absences will not dull the feelings you have for one another.

WEDDING DATES

"Marry on Monday for health, Tuesday for wealth, Wednesday the best day of all . . . " The month and day that you wed holds particular portent for your married life to come—your future health, wealth, and happiness can be determined by this timing. The months themselves hold individual meaning, and within each month are days that are particularly auspicious. Planning wedding events on or near those days is recommended. Choose wisely. . . .

JANUARY

January is named for the Roman god Janus, the god of the doorway. Hence January is seen as the "doorway" to each new year. Marrying in this month signifies that you and your mate will be open to new possibilities throughout your life together.

❖ **Most auspicious dates: 2, 16, 25** ❖

JANUARY 1-15

Marrying early in January reflects your energy and self-reliance. Trust yourself when making wedding arrangements; if you follow your instincts, you will have the ceremony of your dreams.

JANUARY 16-31

A late January wedding will be a social event talked about for years to come.

FEBRUARY

In Scandinavian countries, February is known as "the month of the pearl." Marry in this month and the intensity of your love will be rare and valuable.

❖ **Most auspicious dates: 6, 18, 29** ❖

FEBRUARY 1-15

A marriage between these dates assures children who will be devoted and caring.

FEBRUARY 16-29

Marry in this time period and you will have rare good luck all your lives. A wedding on February 29 of a leap year will bring especially good fortune.

MARCH

March is a month of newfound clarity. Plan your wedding for March and you and your husband will be assured a mutual understanding that will only grow with time.

❖ **Most auspicious dates: 14, 15, 21** ❖

MARCH 1-15

In many cultures, March signifies the beginning of the new year. Marry in the first two weeks of March and your life together will never grow stale.

MARCH 16-31

Usher in spring with a late March wedding, especially on March 21, and you will have an easy time in childbirth.

APPRIL

A wedding in April has the potential to be a fairy-tale event if you are willing to commit the time and energy to planning it.

❖ **Most auspicious dates: 2, 3, 24** ❖

APRIL 1–15

People trust you, and you have the ability to handle a great amount of responsibility. A career in politics may be in your future.

APRIL 16–30

Grace Kelly married Prince Rainier on April 19, 1956. You too have a royal bearing and great beauty. Accentuate it by marrying in this time period.

MAY

May is "the month of mothers." Honor your maternal lineage, and set the stage for motherhood in your own life, by marrying in this month.

❖ **Most auspicious dates: 7, 21, 24** ❖

MAY 1-15

You will receive an unexpected inheritance from a relative you never knew. Spend it on education for your children and the rewards will come back to you several times over.

MAY 16-31

You will have many children and even more grandchildren. Your retirement years will be comfortable and secure.

JUNE

Juno, the goddess of marriage, rules this month. More weddings take place in June than in any other month, and for good reason—Juno ushers in prosperity and joy to couples. Secure your own happiness with June nuptials.

❖ **Most auspicious dates: 4, 12, 24** ❖

JUNE 1-15

A new career opportunity will come your way during the first five years of marriage. Even though it involves a move to a faraway city, you should take it.

JUNE 16-30

You will meet unusual and compelling new friends through charity work you are involved in.

JULY

This month plays host to weddings fit for royalty. On July 29, 1981, Lady Diana Spencer wed Charles, Prince of Wales, in an unforgettable ceremony watched by millions. Stage your own princess wedding in July, and all eyes will be on you.

❖ **Most auspicious dates: 9, 17, 30** ❖

JULY 1–15

You will embark on many business ventures. Most will fail, but the few that do succeed will gain you fame and fortune.

JULY 16–31

You will always have good luck in the summer months.

AUGUST

Marry in August and later in your marriage you will be rewarded for your hard work and commitment.

❖ **Most auspicious dates: 6, 20, 21** ❖

AUGUST 1-15

You will find your greatest happiness in marriage and motherhood.

AUGUST 16-31

Though you can be impulsive, your instincts are usually correct. Continue to follow them. Travel is also in your future—at some point in your life you will live overseas.

SEPTEMBER

An old rhyme states, "Marry in September's shine, your living will be rich and fine." It's true. Plan your wedding for this month and you will garner material possessions as well as much happiness.

❖ **Most auspicious dates: 10, 18, 19** ❖

SEPTEMBER 1–15

You will be blessed with many opportunities throughout your life. Don't hesitate; reach out to them as they are offered to you. Chances you pass up may not come again.

SEPTEMBER 16–30

Keep your heart open. A friend with whom you have had a falling out will try and reconcile things.

OCTOBER

October is an auspicious month for new beginnings. Marry in this month, and later on in life you will find October to be a fortuitous time for starting new ventures and projects.

❖ **Most auspicious dates: 7, 9, 15** ❖

OCTOBER 1-15

Your marriage will be tested in its first few years by an unexpected event—but keep your mate tightly by your side and you will come through even stronger than before.

OCTOBER 16-31

An unexpected prize will be yours; to hasten its coming, enter contests and raffles.

NOVEMBER

November brides tend to blaze their own trails in life. Harness your originality—a unique business prospect may be in your future.

❖ **Most auspicious dates: 5, 20, 27** ❖

NOVEMBER 1-15

You will travel extensively for your chosen career, but your greatest happiness will always come in returning home.

NOVEMBER 16-30

You are very self-reliant. Lean on your partner, friends, and family more, and it will pay off.

DECEMBER

End the year with a wedding in December and it will garner you and your husband protection from harm.

❖ **Most auspicious dates: 4, 10, 31** ❖

DECEMBER 1-15

You have never considered yourself very creative, but be patient: Later in life, you will be the brains behind a new invention.

DECEMBER 16-31

Remember to look forward, not back, and success in all its forms will be yours.

THE PERFECT MATCH

You already know you and your mate are meant for each other—but what do the stars say? Look to the time-tested practice of astrology to determine the best elements of your pairing, and harness them to make your union even stronger. Think also about these matches with regard to the other people (besides your husband-to-be) who will play a key role in your wedding and married life—parents, siblings, bridesmaids, and more. Follow the signs. . . .

THE SIGNS

ARIES _____ March 20–April 18

TAURUS_____April 19–May 20

GEMINI _____May 21–June 20

CANCER_____June 21–July 22

LEO _____ July 23–August 22

VIRGO_____ August 23–September 22

LIBRA _____ September 23–October 22

SCORPIO_____ October 23–November 21

SAGITTARIUS_____ November 22–December 21

CAPRICORN _____ December 22–January 19

AQUARIUS_____January 20–February 18

PISCES_____ February 19–March 19

ARIES

IF THE MATCH IS . . .
ARIES/ARIES

Fire meets fire in this high-energy mix. You have your moments of impatience, yet you are devoted to each other, and you understand each other like no one else can.

ARIES/TAURUS

Aries's generosity plus Taurus's steadiness will make you good parents.

ARIES/GEMINI

Aries loves a good party—and Gemini loves to be the life of the party. You will always entertain each other, and will have a thriving social circle.

ARIES/CANCER

Aries likes to get his or her way; luckily, Cancer is a generous spirit.

ARIES/LEO

You both need to be noticed. If you're able to remember there is room for two in the limelight, you will shine brighter together than apart.

ARIES/VIRGO

Even though Aries may seem hot-tempered, and Virgo likes order and peace, you are both romantics at heart. Keep this in mind when anniversaries come around.

ARIES/LIBRA

Aries is naturally curious, while Libra is quietly intelligent. Tune into each other and you will both learn a great deal.

ARIES/SCORPIO

Aries is lustful, while Scorpio is a master of all things physical. Sparks will fly in the bedroom!

ARIES/SAGITTARIUS

This high-octane pairing will be full of laughter and adventure.

ARIES/CAPRICORN

Aries is fiery, while Capricorn is much more even-keeled. Learn to balance these natures and you will have smooth sailing ahead.

ARIES/AQUARIUS

Aquarius looks to the future; Aries lives in the present. If you understand this dynamic, you can have the best of both worlds.

ARIES/PISCES

This pairing is known for spontaneous fun. Your most enjoyable times will be those that are not planned in advance.

TAURUS

IF THE MATCH IS . . .
TAURUS/TAURUS

You know how stubborn you can be when you think you are right. But you are also stable, grounded, and secure. Learn to give an inch, and you'll get a mile.

TAURUS/GEMINI

Taurus prefers things to stay as they are, where Gemini can change from minute to minute. But embrace your differences—you each can provide a new and interesting dimension for the other.

TAURUS/CANCER

An auspicious pairing indeed. Taurus brings the security that Cancer needs, and Cancer is a nurturing presence for Taurus.

TAURUS/LEO

In this relationship, Leo will be the star who entertains Taurus, and Taurus will be the safe bedrock for Leo to fall back on.

TAURUS/VIRGO

Taurus excels at setting goals and Virgo is a pro at accomplishing them. Divide and conquer!

TAURUS/LIBRA

Libra loves fine food and drink; luckily, Taurus is an excellent cook (or has the potential to be one). Many convivial dinner parties are in your future.

TAURUS/SCORPIO

You both have a secretive side. However, as long as you remain attentive to one another and keep the lines of communication open, this should not pose a problem.

TAURUS/SAGITTARIUS

When you met, sparks flew immediately. Your powerful physical connection will stick around for years.

TAURUS/CAPRICORN

This is a strong pairing—you both long for stability and security, and together you will find it.

TAURUS/AQUARIUS

Aquarius is open to all kinds of people and situations, while Taurus provides a stable home life. Opposites attract in this duo.

TAURUS/PISCES

Stable, rooted Taurus and empathetic, gentle Pisces: You are a solid couple and will make extraordinary parents.

GEMINI

IF THE MATCH IS . . .
GEMINI/GEMINI

You both love variety—make sure you get enough of it together, whether it be through travel, a wide circle of friends, or a number of careers.

GEMINI/CANCER

Gemini is kind, while Cancer is a caretaker; if Gemini can open up to the nurturing Cancer offers, a deep, intense emotional relationship lies ahead.

GEMINI/LEO

Gemini and Leo both have a taste for adventure. For your honeymoon, consider a trek through the rain forest or a camel tour in the desert.

GEMINI/VIRGO

You share the same sense of humor and will laugh together easily and often.

GEMINI/LIBRA

You can talk all night and still have topics to cover. You will never grow bored of each other.

GEMINI/SCORPIO

You are both analysts at heart, and can spend hours trying to figure out motivations behind actions. Make sure you keep communication open between the two of you so suspicions do not flare.

GEMINI/SAGITTARIUS

Your union will work because of your mutual need for independence. Travel together (or even apart) and your bond will stay strong.

GEMINI/CAPRICORN

You are both kind and intelligent. But Capricorn is devoted, while Gemini is more flighty. Work together to find a happy medium.

GEMINI/AQUARIUS

You will need to work on your emotional connection when troubles occur, but you both have the potential to do it. And when the skies are clear, you have a stronger bond than most couples.

GEMINI/PISCES

Gemini is upbeat and high-energy while Pisces is more low-key. Remember that you do not have to do everything together; oftentimes some space is good for the relationship.

CANCER

CANCER/CANCER

You can be clingy, but luckily you both have this trait. Cling to each other!

CANCER/LEO

Leo will go out and seek fame and fortune, while Cancer is always there to lend reassurance and support.

CANCER/VIRGO

The calm practicality of Virgo helps Cancer feel secure, and Virgo welcomes Cancer's caring intuition.

CANCER/LIBRA

Cancer and Libra are both intensely loyal beings. You will never have a reason to doubt each other.

CANCER/SCORPIO

You both feel things deeply. Harness your powerful intuition and empathy to care for each other throughout your lives.

CANCER/SAGITTARIUS

Cancer wants to possess, while Sagittarius shies away from being contained. You will each have to give a little, and the marriage will work.

CANCER/CAPRICORN

Cancer's empathy and Capricorn's quiet leadership will make you excellent parents. Several years into your marriage, you will deliberate over whether to try for another child. Take the plunge; it will be the right decision.

CANCER/AQUARIUS

You both have a taste for adventure and spontaneity. It's likely that you will move and change careers several times throughout your lives.

CANCER/PISCES

Your combined sensitivity and empathy is unparalleled. Neither of you needs feel unprotected when you are together.

LEO

LEO/LEO

You both crave attention; remember the importance of spending a little quiet time together. You will emerge renewed, and will find yourselves ready to take on even more challenges.

LEO/VIRGO

Leo's confidence and Virgo's attention to detail make this a good coupling for future entrepreneurship.

LEO/LIBRA

Libra likes big personalities, while Leo is a constant entertainer. You will draw much enjoyment from each other.

LEO/SCORPIO

Both passionate, Leo is an open flame while Scorpio is a glowing ember. It's a complicated relationship, but it can work. Remember to support each other in all your endeavors.

LEO/SAGITTARIUS

You are a passionate couple. Things will go better if Leo remembers to let Sagittarius take the spotlight every now and then.

LEO/CAPRICORN

Leo will be the outwardly dominant member of the pairing, but Capricorn brings a diligent, family-oriented streak to the mix that will serve you both well.

LEO/AQUARIUS

Together, you are passionate and romantic—a rare lucky combination.

LEO/PISCES

Loyal Leo and expressive Pisces make a good team, especially when it comes to marriage.

VIRGO

IF THE MATCH IS . . .
VIRGO/VIRGO

While you have been accused of being a perfectionist, you know how to do the job right. Luckily, your fellow Virgo feels the same way!

VIRGO/LIBRA

Do not make hasty decisions. Virgo is a planner, and Libra does best when deliberating before coming to a conclusion. The combination of your strong wills can be an immensely powerful force and will bring the two of you great satisfaction.

VIRGO/SCORPIO

Virgo keeps his or her lustiness under wraps, while Scorpio wears it on his or her sleeve—but you've both got it, so use it!

VIRGO/SAGITTARIUS

Your connection is both mental and physical—not everyone is so lucky.

VIRGO/CAPRICORN

Together, you are organized, practical, and diligent. This union will stand the test of time.

VIRGO/AQUARIUS

Aquarius's openness will help organized Virgo lighten up, and Virgo can serve as a grounding presence for Aquarius.

VIRGO/PISCES

Pisces is governed by emotions, while Virgo relies on logic. But don't worry. Each relationship needs a bit of both qualities.

LIBRA

IF THE MATCH IS ...
LIBRA/LIBRA

One of Libra's greatest desires is to find a soul mate. Now that you have done so, you will take to married life easily.

LIBRA/SCORPIO

You both thrive on romance. In the early years of marriage, it will come easily, but be sure to cultivate it over the years so the spark stays alive.

LIBRA/SAGITTARIUS

You both appreciate the finer things in life. You will have a luxurious home and many beautiful possessions.

LIBRA/CAPRICORN

You both long for old-fashioned romance. Bring flowers, go out dancing, write love letters to one another; you will stoke the fires of love.

LIBRA/AQUARIUS

The spiritual connection you have with each other is rare and powerful.

LIBRA/PISCES

Libra will need to get more comfortable with emotions, because Pisces thrives on expressiveness—but this obstacle can be fairly easily overcome.

SCORPIO

IF THE MATCH IS...
SCORPIO/SCORPIO

You are too intense for some people, but so is your fellow Scorpio. For each other, you are a perfect fit.

SCORPIO/SAGITTARIUS

Sagittarius and Scorpio both have hidden wild sides. Tap into them and there is no telling what magic may come of it.

SCORPIO/CAPRICORN

Scorpio's deep emotion lets Capricorn express true feelings, and Capricorn allows Scorpio to feel safe.

SCORPIO/AQUARIUS

Both Aquarius and Scorpio possess deep wells of creativity;
tap into these together and use them to your advantage.

SCORPIO/PISCES

Your intuitive natures will complement each other—Scorpio
will teach a mate to be a careful listener, and Pisces will
show a partner how to express the best of him or herself.

SAGITTARIUS

IF THE MATCH IS . . .
SAGITTARIUS/SAGITTARIUS

You have common hopes and dreams for the future, and you understand each other perfectly. You will disagree only on rare occasions.

SAGITTARIUS/CAPRICORN

Sagittarius can be wary of commitment, but with Capricorn in the picture, this should not be a problem.

SAGITTARIUS/AQUARIUS

Together you make a lively couple—you will have many friends and always be surrounded by admirers.

SAGITTARIUS/PISCES

To outsiders, you may seem to be flighty dreamers—but share your dreams with each other and they can become reality.

CAPRICORN

IF THE MATCH IS . . .
CAPRICORN/CAPRICORN

Capricorns are natural workhorses. Once you commit to something together, especially a business or other enterprise, there is no stopping you.

CAPRICORN/AQUARIUS

Harness Aquarius's forward-thinking, free-spirited nature and combine it with the practical, grounded side of Capricorn to create a force to be reckoned with.

CAPRICORN/PISCES

Pisces brings kindness and compassion to the mix; Capricorn provides stability and grounding.

AQUARIUS

IF THE MATCH IS . . .
AQUARIUS/AQUARIUS

You are both free spirits, and you hate to play by the rules. Remember that it doesn't matter what others think of you as long as you are in love.

AQUARIUS/PISCES

Pisces is ruled by emotions, which can be a good match for free-spirited Aquarius. But Aquarius must be willing to relax a bit and accept Pisces' kindness and love.

PISCES

IF THE MATCH IS . . .
PISCES/PISCES

The rest of the world just melts away when you are alone together. Tune into the outside world when you need to, but in your home life, revel in your unique and special connection.

FLOWER GIRL

Flowers have long served to perfume and beautify our surroundings. And they are rich in meaning as well, especially when it comes to weddings. Brides in ancient Greece held bunches of herbs for the purpose of fending off evil spirits, and Roman brides carried sheaves of wheat to symbolize fertility. The bridal bouquets of today have become much more elaborate, but no less important. What flowers do you favor? Your fortune lies within. . . .

FLOWERS

From aster to zinnia, you have many choices when it comes to wedding flowers—and these choices can bring you luck, happiness, and true love.

ASTER

Legend has it that an aster first bloomed when the constellation Virgo dropped stardust to earth. Choose asters, and you and your love will travel far and wide and see great lands.

Best used for: Accent flowers in all bouquets, cake decorations

Most auspicious in: September

CALLA LILY

You have unparalleled beauty. Although many men desire you, you and your mate will love each other with great ardor.

Best used for: Bridal bouquet, boutonnieres

Most auspicious in: December, January, February

CARNATION

Carnations augur true bliss in marriage. Your husband's profound admiration of you will never fade.

Best used for: Bridal bouquet, bridesmaids' bouquets, boutonnieres
Most auspicious in: January, June

CHRYSANTHEMUM

Your optimistic outlook on life will ensure happiness. Your mate's innate cheerfulness is a very good match for you.

Best used for: Bridal bouquet, table centerpieces, corsages
Most auspicious in: September, October, November

DAFFODIL

Give your husband-to-be a daffodil to wear on your wedding day, and he will always be chivalrous and kind.

Best used for: Boutonnieres, bridal bouquets
Most auspicious in: December, January, February, March

DAHLIA

You and your mate will take part in an action that will win you the gratitude of thousands.

Best used for: Bridal bouquet, table centerpieces, ceremony decorations, hair ornamentation

Most auspicious in: August, September, October

DAISY

Daisies, in olden days, were carried by unmarried women to show that they returned a suitor's affection. Choose daisies, and you and your love will always be true to one another. Wear a daisy in your left stocking and you will give birth early in marriage.

Best used for: Flower girl's basket, hair ornamentation, bridesmaids' bouquets, cake decorations

Most auspicious in: July, August, September, October

FREESIA

You and your beloved will lead an innocent life, untouched by worry or harm.

Best used for: Bridal bouquet, table accents, cake decorations
Most auspicious in: May, June, July

GARDENIA

Still waters run deep: The strong mutual attraction you have as newlyweds will never fade.

Best used for: Table centerpieces, table accents, boutonnieres, corsages
Most auspicious in: March, May, October

HYDRANGEA

You and your husband will become devoted to a particular cause and will spend much of your time and energies working in pursuit of it. It will do much to strengthen your union.

Best used for: Table centerpieces, bridal bouquets, bridesmaids' bouquets, boutonnieres
Most auspicious in: July, August, November

IRIS

You will develop a great eloquence, and it will win you fame and fortune.

Best used for: Ceremony decorations, table centerpieces, table accents
Most auspicious in: April, May, June

LILY

You have a regal quality and may seem standoffish at times, but your loyalty runs deep. As the years go by, friends will know you as a steady rock in times of trouble.

Best used for: Ceremony decorations, table centerpieces, bridal bouquet

Most auspicious in: February, March, April

LILY OF THE VALLEY

This delicate flower signifies a return of happiness. It is true that there have been rough periods in your life—but rejoice; there will be smooth sailing from here on out.

Best used for: Bridal bouquet, bridesmaids' bouquets, table accents

Most auspicious in: March, May

NARCISSUS

This bloom, especially the paperwhite narcissus, will bring you the respect that you greatly deserve.

Best used for: Table accents, cake decorations
Most auspicious in: December, March, April

ORCHID

You and your husband will always be passionate about each other, and you will live in great luxury. If your husband eats an orchid petal on the wedding day, you will be blessed with many children.

Best used for: Table centerpieces, boutonnieres, corsages, hair ornamentation
Most auspicious in: December, August, September

PEONY

The springtime will always be a season of great happiness
and renewal for your family.

Best used for: Bridal bouquet, ceremony decorations
Most auspicious in: March, April, May

ROSE

Roses in your bouquet will mean a future life of small kind-
nesses bestowed upon you by strangers. Pale pink roses
mean that only one person truly understands your heart—
your groom. Red and white roses together symbolize the
unity in your marriage, while yellow roses signify the deep
friendship the two of you will share.

Best used for: Bridal bouquet, table centerpieces, corsages
Most auspicious in: June

SNAPDRAGON

If you carry snapdragons down the aisle, you will most likely give birth to your first child in the springtime.

Best used for: Bridal bouquet, table centerpieces
Most auspicious in: March, April, May

SUNFLOWER

Your children will adore you. Later in life, you will meet another child, unrelated to you, who will also become unfailingly devoted to you.

Best used for: Table centerpieces, ceremony decorations
Most auspicious in: May, June, October, November

SWEET PEA

The lasting fragrance of sweet pea symbolizes the ongoing enjoyment you and your mate will gain from each other.

Best used for: Bridal bouquet, flower girl's basket, table accents
Most auspicious in: April, May

TUBEROSE

Your wit and charm will be legendary among your group
of friends.

Best used for: Ceremony decorations, cake decorations, table accents
Most auspicious in: June, July, August, September

TULIP

You and your beloved have a bond so strong that nothing
in your life will be able to shake it. As you pass your
twentieth anniversary, this bond will grow even stronger.
Carrying red tulips, in particular, signifies your devotion
to each other.

Best used for: Table centerpieces, bridal bouquet,
bridesmaids' bouquets
Most auspicious in: April, May

VIOLET

You will be known for your unfailingly kind and patient nature.

Best used for: Boutonnieres, corsages, ceremony decorations
Most auspicious in: February

ZINNIA

You and your love will be happiest when surrounded by your wide circle of friends.

Best used for: Bridesmaids' bouquets, table centerpieces
Most auspicious in: July, August, September

PLANTS AND HERBS

In ancient times, young girls dropped herbs in the walkway ahead of a bride to aid in fertility in the marriage. Herbs and other plants are still powerful today. Consider one of these as an accent to your other flowers, or in place of them:

ACORN _____prosperity and power

BASIL _____long-lasting love

BAY _____ fame

CHAMOMILE _____ wisdom

CHERRY BLOSSOM____ feminine power and beauty

CHIVE _____good luck

DILL_____ good cheer

IVY _____ everlasting love

PARSLEY_____merriment

ROSEMARY _____remembrance

SAGE _____ wisdom

FLOWERS, MONTH BY MONTH

Each month of the year has a representative flower. Choose this flower for the month you will be married in and good luck will surely come your way.

JANUARY_____ Carnation

FEBRUARY_____Violet

MARCH_____Daffodil

APRIL _____ Sweet Pea/Daisy

MAY_____Lily of the Valley

JUNE _____Rose

JULY_____ Larkspur

AUGUST_____Gladiolus/Poppy

SEPTEMBER _____Aster/Morning Glory

OCTOBER _____Calendula

NOVEMBER_____Chrysanthemum

DECEMBER _____ Narcissus/Holly

THE COLOR SCHEME

The color scheme you choose for your wedding is a reflection of you—more than you may realize, in fact. In this section, uncover the meanings behind colors, and learn how certain colors can be most fortuitous when used in combination with others, or in particular parts of the wedding. If the exact colors you were envisioning for your big day are not mentioned here, see the colors that are close by in the spectrum; it is likely that the portents will be similar. Prepare to make your wedding day a truly colorful affair. . . .

WARM COLORS

Reds, oranges, yellows, and their associated hues are bold, energetic, vivid, and convey passion and optimism. Welcome the same qualities into your life by choosing warm colors for your wedding palette.

BURGUNDY

Your attention to detail is one of your strongest traits. Because of it, your wedding will be a flawless event—friends will marvel at how you pulled it all off.

Best used for: Invitations, accents on groom's and groomsmen's suits, ceremony decorations
Most fortuitous when used in combination with: Silver, mint green, pale blue

CORAL

You are not afraid to take risks. Go after what you desire in life; you will very likely attain it.

Best used for: Seaside ceremonies and receptions; table settings, invitations
Most fortuitous when used in combination with: Teal, chocolate brown, yellow

ORANGE

Your sunny disposition cheers everyone around you, and your optimism will carry you over any rough spots.

Best used for: Flowers, ceremony decorations
Most fortuitous when used in combination with: Red, brown

PEACH

Peach accents in a wedding, especially on a gown, mean you will be known for great beauty in your later years.

Best used for: Flowers (especially bouquets), table settings, dresses for flower girls
Most fortuitous when used in combination with: Cream, scarlet

RED

You are passionate about everything you do. As you grow older, you will use this passion, along with a newfound boldness and determination, to start a wildly successful business venture.

Best used for: Evening weddings; flowers, bridesmaids' dresses
Most fortuitous when used in combination with: Baby blue, aqua, chocolate brown

YELLOW

You are optimistic, cheerful, and a loyal friend. You and your wedding attendants will be close for life.

Best used for: Summer weddings; flowers, dresses for flower girls
Most fortuitous when used in combination with: Silver, cream, white

COOL COLORS

The cool colors—greens, blues, purples, and their combinations—are soothing and calming. The colors of nature, they also speak of renewal and growth.

AQUA

You are a true original. Don't ever let anyone try and tone you down.

Best used for: Seaside or poolside weddings; invitations, ceremony and reception decorations

Most fortuitous when used in combination with: Pink, chocolate brown

BABY BLUE

Baby blue is a calm, soothing color—and the bride who uses it in her ceremony will be blessed with a marriage of peace and stability.

Best used for: Winter weddings; bridesmaids' dresses, accents on groom's and groomsmen's suits

Most fortuitous when used in combination with: Navy blue, red, burgundy

FOREST GREEN

Constancy is your calling card. Your dependability and steadfastness will come in handy in marriage and parenthood.

Best used for: Evening weddings; invitations, accents on groom's and groomsmen's suits

Most fortuitous when used in combination with: Pink, baby blue, cream

KELLY GREEN

Your patience has always paid off for you. Continue to rely on it, and you will have an easy path through life.

Best used for: Invitations, table settings

Most fortuitous when used in combination with: Black, white, aqua

LAVENDER

Lavender stands for enchantment. Use it in your ceremony and your husband will be as taken with you fifty years from now as he is on your wedding day.

Best used for: Wedding cake, flowers
Most fortuitous when used in combination with: Navy blue, red

MAGENTA

You are a strong woman who knows what she wants. You've got your man, and the wedding of your dreams is ahead.

Best used for: Invitations, bridesmaids' dresses
Most fortuitous when used in combination with: Black, lime green, brown

NAVY BLUE

The color blue on a wedding day symbolizes tradition and stability. And as the Old English rhyme goes, "Married in blue, he will always be true."

Best used for: Invitations, suits for groom and groomsmen
Most fortuitous when used in combination with: Silver, cream, sage green, white

PALE PINK

Grace is one of your hallmarks—but you also know how to have fun.

Best used for: Flowers (especially bouquets), accents for groom's and groomsmen's suits, wedding dress accent, wedding cake
Most fortuitous when used in combination with: Chocolate brown, navy blue

PURPLE

You carry yourself like royalty. As the years go by, your elegance and sophistication will become widely appreciated. But retain your air of mystery, for it is a large part of your winning charm.

Best used for: Invitations, table accents, ceremony decorations

Most fortuitous when used in combination with: Gray, silver, burgundy

ROYAL BLUE

This is a color for a modern-day Cinderella story. If you fell in love at first sight, royal blue is a fitting tribute.

Best used for: Ceremony decorations, invitations

Most fortuitous when used in combination with: Gold, yellow, baby blue

THE NEUTRALS

The neutral colors of black, brown, gray, cream, and white speak of stability and earthiness. Use them on their own, or to bring a grounding presence to other brighter colors in your palette.

BLACK

You are wildly sophisticated and you lead by example. Continue to be a trendsetter; don't ever follow the pack.

Best used for: Evening weddings; suits for groom and groomsmen, invitations

Most fortuitous when used in combination with: All shades of red

CHOCOLATE BROWN

You are artistic, and will gain fame and recognition later in life for your talents.

Best used for: Bridesmaids' dresses, invitations, table settings
Most fortuitous when used in combination with: Mint green, coral, aqua

CREAM

Cream carries all the elegance and refinement of white, but it—and you—also has a softer side.

Best used for: Wedding dress, invitations, ceremony decorations
Most fortuitous when used in combination with: Lavender, violet, blue

GRAY

You are a benevolent soul, and find your greatest pleasure in helping others.

Best used for: Accents for groom's and groomsmen's suits, invitations
Most fortuitous when used in combination with: Pale pink, butter yellow, royal blue

WHITE

White, in all its shades, is the most traditional wedding color. Brides who choose it are elegant and refined. Used with the color red, white forecasts a union that will stand the test of time.

Best used for: Wedding dress, table settings, invitations, flowers
Most fortuitous when used in combination with: Red, forest green

THE METALLICS

Metallic colors like to show themselves off. Dazzle your guests by giving a metallic a starring role, or use one sparingly as an accent to add a touch of glamour and excitement.

CHAMPAGNE

You will travel far and wide and enjoy exposure to many cultures.

Best used for: Bridesmaids' dresses, reception decorations
Most fortuitous when used in combination with: Copper, magenta, burgundy

COPPER

You will be a breath of fresh air in your future husband's family, and you will have no problem using your powers of diplomacy to smooth over any misunderstandings with the in-laws.

Best used for: Bridesmaids' dresses, invitations, table settings
Most fortuitous when used in combination with: Aqua, dark teal, champagne

GOLD

The world is your oyster. Whatever path you choose to take will be a successful one.

Best used for: Table settings, reception decorations
Most fortuitous when used in combination with: Royal blue, navy blue, burgundy

PLATINUM

Be at your ease; financial troubles will never darken your door.

Best used for: Evening weddings; accents for groom's and groomsmen's suits, bridesmaids' dresses, reception decorations
Most fortuitous when used in combination with: Blue of all shades

SILVER

The glitz and glamour represented by silver will rub off on any bride who chooses it.

Best used for: Winter weddings; table settings, invitations
Most fortuitous when used in combination with: Maroon, pale blue

RINGS AND THINGS

The engagement ring and the wedding band: Two of the smallest elements in a wedding, they hold immense significance. Folklore has it that the fourth finger contains within it a vein that leads directly to the heart—and that is why the engagement ring and wedding band are most often worn on that finger.

On the wedding day, you will most likely be wearing your engagement ring, and by the end of the ceremony you will also bear a wedding band. Both of these represent the commitment you and your love have made to each other. But the type of precious metal and the gemstones involved, on your rings and in other jewelry you may be wearing on the day of the nuptials, can tell you still more about your future. . . .

GEMSTONES

Gemstones carry within them powerful meaning. If one of the following stones is a part of your engagement ring, read on to see what fortune will be coming your way. Or wear one or a combination of these stones on the day of your nuptials and choose the luck you most desire.

AMBER

Amber catches negativity and can change it to positive. Wear it if you have any anxiety at all about the wedding day or the ceremony itself. Or give an amber charm to a bridesmaid who is feeling particularly nervous or depressed.

AMETHYST

Amethyst calms the mind and brings clarity and wisdom. However, its most powerful aspect is its ability to help one let go of the past and embrace the future. Wear it if you need an extra push from your single life into your married one.

AQUAMARINE

Aquamarine brings courage and sharpens the intuition. It also offers protection from harm. Wear it to draw strength to yourself on the wedding day.

CARNELIAN

Carnelian banishes envy, fear, and sadness. Keep your spirits light with a piece of jewelry that showcases carnelian.

CITRINE

Particularly suited for go-getter personalities, citrine attracts success and wealth and holds on to it.

DIAMOND

Diamond is a protector—it represents strength and eternity. You may likely have a diamond as part of your engagement ring—but it does not hurt to amplify its powers by pairing with a matching necklace or earrings on the big day.

EMERALD

Emerald is omnipotent—it strikes down sadness, brings peace, heals, gives patience, and provides balance. It seals marriages and families. The love it watches over lasts forever.

GARNET

Garnet is a purifying gemstone. It also brings constancy and stability. Wear a garnet ring and you will be untouched by all doubt on the wedding day.

HEMATITE

Hematite calms anxiety, and brings self-awareness. Use it on your wedding day and you will be at your best during the nuptials and the celebration afterward.

JADE

Jade stands for prosperity and serenity. Green jade in particular heals the heart and binds lovers together. Wisdom and protection come to all couples who wear it.

ONYX

Onyx, and black onyx in particular, provides grounding and stability, and also augurs productivity.

OPAL

Opal represents hope. It also has the power to amplify and clarify buried feelings and desires—wear it on your wedding day and your vows to your husband will come easily and ring true.

PEARL

On a wedding day, pearls stand in for a bride's real tears, ensuring her a future life with little sadness and much joy. If possible, borrow pearls from a relative who has had a very happy life. White pearls also represent purity, modesty, and innocence, while gold and black pearls forecast prosperity.

PERIDOT

Peridot ushers in understanding and acceptance, helps with openness, and relieves anger, fear, and jealousy. It also increases one's inner strength—an important quality on a wedding day.

ROSE QUARTZ

Rose quartz opens the heart and allows for the free exchange of love. Worn on the wedding day, it enhances the beauty of the bride. It has also been used in love rituals for thousands of years because it aids with passion in the physical relationship.

RUBY

Rubies attract wisdom, heighten self-confidence, and allow their wearers to face old fears and put them behind. Wear rubies, and you will be adventurous and also protected against misfortune in your adventures.

SAPPHIRE

Wearing sapphires brings great insight and intuition, both into the future and into the minds of others. Wear it on your wedding day and communication between you and your husband will always be smooth and easy. Peace and joy will be a hallmark of your love.

TIGER'S EYE

Tiger's eye brings clarity of thinking, and takes anxiety and fear and changes it to confidence and action. If you need a boost of motivation, wear a tiger's eye.

TOPAZ

Topaz offers strength, physical stamina, and focus. It lessens anxiety, tiredness, moodiness, and nervousness. To a union of two lovers, it offers fidelity.

TURQUOISE

Turquoise is a grounding stone. Its color comes from the blue of the sky and the green of the earth, and as such it can signify prosperity and wisdom. Wear it during your wedding and you will feel secure and safe.

BIRTHSTONES

Another way to draw good fortune to oneself on a wedding day is to wear one's birthstone. It will amplify the already-existing powers of the stone.

JANUARY_____Garnet or Rose Quartz

FEBRUARY_____Amethyst or Onyx

MARCH_____Aquamarine or Bloodstone

APRIL _____Diamond

MAY_____Emerald

JUNE _____ Pearl or Moonstone

JULY_____ Ruby or Carnelian

AUGUST_____Peridot or Sardonyx

SEPTEMBER _____ Sapphire or Lapis

OCTOBER _____ Opal or Tourmaline

NOVEMBER_____ Topaz or Citrine

DECEMBER _____ Turquoise or Tanzanite

PRECIOUS METALS

What metals are your engagement ring and wedding band made from? Read on to discover their portent.

GOLD

Gold will bring good health; wearing a gold band will also increase your inner strength and willpower.

WHITE GOLD

Choose white gold for your wedding bands, and a close friend of yours will meet her future husband at your wedding.

PLATINUM

Wearing a wedding band made of this scarce metal will garner you protection from harm.

SILVER

You are artistic and creative; cultivate this talent and it will someday bring you great happiness and comfortable wealth.

THE WEDDING BAND

Will you engrave your wedding bands, or will you and your mate decide against wearing wedding bands? Both choices speak volumes about you.

ENGRAVING

Whether it is your names or initials, the wedding date, a phrase or line of verse that holds meaning for you and your mate, or a symbol that represents you both, engraving on the band is a special way to accentuate the commitment that the wedding band symbolizes. A couple who decides to engrave their bands holds their lineage dear. They also share a sense of privacy and intimacy in their marriage.

NO WEDDING BAND

Forgoing wedding bands altogether is an unconventional step, but it makes the marriage and the bond no less strong. You and your mate are independent, but also trust in each other deeply. Continue to do so and your love will know no boundaries.

DRESS THE PART

For thousands of years, women have donned their best dresses for their wedding day. The wedding dress is one of the most personal choices a bride will make—and perhaps the most beautiful dress she will ever wear. The one you choose, and the accessories you select to accompany the dress, show your personal blend of style, elegance, and grace. You've dreamed of this day, and dreamed of the dress—now read on to see what else your choice reflects. . . .

SILHOUETTES

From the sweeping grandeur of a ball gown to the no-nonsense close fit of a sheath, the silhouette of the dress you wear truly makes a personal statement, and holds meaning as well.

A-LINE/PRINCESS

Like the letter A, a bride in this dress likes to stand up front
and be recognized. You are the master of your own destiny.
Don't ever settle for second best.

SHEATH

You are a born leader. Your personality is magnetic and
admirers and followers will always surround you. Treat
people with kindness and you will go even further.

EMPIRE

You are a free thinker and have a real ability to
inspire others. Later in life, you will be at the forefront of
social change.

BALL GOWN

You love deeply but have a tendency to be reserved. Work on your expressiveness and your relationships with others will only flourish.

MERMAID

You have always attracted the attention of the opposite sex—but luckily for your husband, once you give your love to one person, you will always be true.

LENGTHS

Long, short, or somewhere in between—the perfect length for your dress is up to you, as it reflects your unique personality.

FLOOR-LENGTH

You are known for your poise in difficult situations. You tend to be serious, but have a playful side that others delight in seeing. You love deeply and will be a devoted partner to your mate.

ANKLE-LENGTH

You are a model of discretion. Friends will rely on you to keep their secrets, and you never disappoint. Keenly observant, you notice things that others do not, and the conclusions you draw from these observations are nearly always accurate.

COCKTAIL LENGTH OR TEA LENGTH

You have high ideals. Although it takes much to please you, when you are satisfied you are quick to lavish praise. You are intelligent and studious and would do well to dedicate yourself to academic pursuits.

KNEE-LENGTH

Your nature is easy and casual; your feathers are not easily ruffled. Your generosity is one of your finest traits. Keep on giving of yourself; your selflessness will pay off.

COLOR

Traditionally, brides have worn all white, but today they are accentuating their wedding-day outfits with splashes of color, whether they be shoes, jewelry, hairpieces, a sash on the dress itself, or more. If you set off your stunning gown with color, here is what meaning lies within.

RED

Red commands attention. It represents confidence and an outgoing nature. It is also the color of greatest passion and happiness.

ORANGE

Orange is vibrant, but more friendly than red. It speaks of energy and liveliness but also has a soothing side to it.

YELLOW

The color of the sun, yellow signifies hope and friendship.

GREEN

Green stands for stability and balance, but also speaks of growth and freshness.

BLUE

Blue means importance, intelligence, and unity. It is the color of confidence.

PURPLE

Purple has both a sacred and a regal feeling. It heightens and shows off imagination and creativity.

ACCESSORIES AND EMBELLISHMENTS

Accessories to the bridal gown can also hold special meaning, and are often steeped in history. For example, legend has it that veils first began to be worn at weddings when, in the 18th century, a young man walked past the house of George Washington and saw his daughter, Nelly, sitting in the front window, her face framed by a lace curtain. He was instantly taken with her, and when they married a short time afterward, she wore a lace-trimmed veil to recreate the effect.

EMBROIDERY

Embroidery on a wedding dress foretells a life that will be enriched by the arts. If your dress is embroidered, when you can afford it, consider becoming a patron to an up-and-coming artist who needs your support.

GLOVES

Gloves are elegant and theatrical, but they also represent a bride who is careful and gentle with her loved ones. She will make a wonderful mother.

LACE

Lace detailing on a gown befits a bride who is a romantic at heart, and augurs enduring love for the couple.

PEARLS

Pearls on a wedding dress forecast an innocent life, with little trouble or strife. The wearer, however, will be wise and dignified.

RIBBONS

Ribbons woven into the wedding gown signify that the bride is compassionate and empathetic. Concerned about causes, she stands up for what she believes in.

TRAIN

A train behind a wedding gown is a regal touch. The bride who wears one has ambition and shrewdness, but can also show a great amount of kindness and sympathy toward those in need.

VEIL

It's no secret that a veil can really make a bride look the part. The bride who wears a veil has a mysterious way about her, but she also holds tradition dear. Her home and family will be of paramount importance to her.

SOMETHING OLD . . .

"Something old, something new, something borrowed, something blue, and a sixpence in her shoe." This old saying still holds weight today, as brides seek out old, new, borrowed, and blue items to incorporate into their wedding days. Here are some particularly auspicious ones.

OLD

❖ A locket owned by the bride's grandmother

❖ A love letter sent by the bride's or groom's father to his future wife

❖ A pair of vintage gloves

❖ A photograph of the bride's grandparents at their wedding

NEW

❖ A new piece of jewelry for the bride to wear on the wedding day

❖ The key to the bride and groom's new home

❖ A new handbag purchased specifically for the wedding

BORROWED

❖ The groom's father's or grandfather's pocket watch or wristwatch

❖ A brooch owned by the bride's mother

❖ A handkerchief from either side of the family

❖ A wedding gown from the bride's mother or other family member

BLUE

❖ A blue sash on the wedding gown

❖ Blue dresses for bridesmaids or the flower girl

❖ A sapphire in the wedding jewelry

SIXPENCE

❖ A literal sixpence piece is most fortuitous (placed in the bride's left shoe, it will bring good fortune and prosperity), but if this coin cannot be found, an old coin from a country of the bride's heritage will serve as an adequate stand-in.

WHATEVER THE WEATHER

When planning a wedding, there are many details to control. Like it or not, the weather is not one of them. But put your trust in fate, and the weather portents that follow, and you will find that whatever the weather, as long as you have your mate by your side, happy times are in store. . . .

THE ENGAGEMENT

One of the happiest days of your life can be the day you become engaged. And the weather on that day can forecast even more happiness.

SUNSHINE/CLEAR SKIES

An unobstructed sky symbolizes a clear future. It is a very favorable sign for the day of an engagement.

CLOUDS

If you get engaged on a cloudy day, this suggests that at least one friend or family member will have trouble accepting your engagement. Trust your intuition when you deal with the situation, and things will soon clear up.

RAIN

Rain around the time of an engagement signals creativity is on the horizon. Bask in the excitement of being newly betrothed, but also consider using this newfound energy to do some early wedding planning.

SNOW

Virgin snow represents new beginnings—and as such is a very auspicious sign for an engagement. If the snow is falling when the engagement happens, you will find a new way of looking at an old problem, and this will bring you the resolution you have been hoping for.

THE ENGAGEMENT PARTY

Friends and family will gather to celebrate your engagement—what do the skies have in store?

SUNSHINE/CLEAR SKIES

Clear skies for an engagement party augur a good time will be had by all!

CLOUDS

Clouds obscuring the sun indicate a circumstance in your life that seems worse than it actually is. Be patient—everything will turn out fine in the end. If the sun is shining through clouds, the resolution will come sooner rather than later.

RAIN

Rain has cleansing properties. If you have had a falling out with a close friend or family member around the time of your engagement party, keep your fingers crossed: Rain on the day of the party will enable you to patch things up more easily.

SNOW

Clean, white snow for the engagement party signals a future truth-telling: Expect someone at the party to let you in on a confidence.

THE BACHELORETTE PARTY

You will have your close friends and family around you—read on to see what the weather portends, and then get ready to celebrate!

SUNSHINE/CLEAR SKIES

Sunshine and clear skies for the bachelorette party forecast a transformation. What it most likely means is that you will let your hair down for the festivities and have a great time!

CLOUDS

If it is cloudy around the time of the bachelorette party, this may represent an underlying tension, perhaps between you and one of your bridesmaids. Clear up any misunderstandings before the party begins, and the tension will surely dissipate.

RAIN

Rain for a bachelorette celebration: A night of surprises lies ahead!

SNOW

Snow can symbolize emotions that are being repressed. Search inside yourself, and if there is something you need to say to someone, now is the time to say it. You will be happy you did.

THE REHEARSAL DINNER

The wedding is just around the corner. Look to the weather for signs, and you will be well prepared for the big day.

SUNSHINE/CLEAR SKIES

Sunshine signifies a change in your near future—yes, you are getting married, but other big and fortunate change is also on the horizon.

CLOUDS

White clouds mean positive energy, while darker clouds point to negative thinking. If the skies are dark, buck up— your wedding will turn things around.

RAIN

Rain replenishes and renews, and also augurs fertility; if it rains on the night before your wedding, children may be in your near future.

SNOW

Falling snow on the eve of the wedding means you will soon get a letter—most likely a love letter from your future husband. Anticipate it with pleasure, for it will bring you happiness and good luck.

THE WEDDING

Your wedding day has arrived! Don't worry about the weather—just let fate take its course and all things will work out for the best.

SUNSHINE/CLEAR SKIES

A wedding day full of sunshine means your union will be a calm one, with very little strain or strife. Tuck a lock of your beloved's hair under your pillow on the eve of your wedding and the sun will surely shine on the big day.

CLOUDS

Bright, fluffy clouds in a clear sky symbolize hopes and dreams that are attainable with just a little work. The more clouds, the better—they also signify success in love.

RAIN

While many brides dread a rainy day for their wedding, the truth is that rain on a wedding day is a very auspicious sign. Sprinkles signify that you will be financially secure—and rain showers foretell great prosperity. A thunderstorm is an even better thing, and a rainbow after a storm on a wedding day is the best omen of all.

SNOW

Snow brings another meaning to the term "white wedding." It augurs a marriage of openness and sharing, and indicates that any current obstacles in your path will soon be melting away.

TOKENS OF LOVE

All brides know the importance of "something old, something new, something borrowed, and something blue." But it goes beyond that well-worn phrase. Other symbols, if incorporated into the nuptials, or if come upon by chance over the course of the wedding day, can hold great portent. Look for these signs on your wedding day and see what good fortune will be yours. . . .

BEARD

Seeing a man with a beard at your wedding augurs longevity for you and your mate. If the bearded man is someone you have not met before, it is an even better sign.

BEES

Bees symbolize industry. If you see bees in the air at your wedding ceremony, it is a sign that you will be successful in business. Embroider a bee on a handkerchief and give it to your fiancé. If he keeps it in his pocket on the wedding day, you will attract wealth.

BOOKS

Books augur the contentment that can come from potential fulfilled. Give books as favors to your guests or gifts to your bridesmaids, and they will be able to complete tasks they have been putting off.

BUTTERFLY

Seeing butterflies at a wedding is a harbinger of pleasant times ahead. Butterflies also represent the human soul and its ability to adapt to change. If a butterfly alights on a wedding guest during your ceremony, you will have happiness in your marriage beyond your wildest expectations.

CANDLE

A lighted candle has a healing power. Light candles near the space where you are getting married and those close to you who are hurting will find comfort.

CLOCKS

A clock in the room where you are getting dressed for the ceremony is a fortuitous sign; it represents order and structure in your life to come. The higher the number of the hour the clock is approaching, the more this portent holds true.

COINS

During the ceremony, have your mother carry a gold coin and your father a silver one, and luck will always come your way.

DOVES

Doves mate for life. Release a pair of white doves after your ceremony and your husband will always be faithful.

DUCKS

Swimming ducks can portend luck with money, while flying ducks symbolize great achievement. Have your wedding near a pond where ducks live to draw this luck to you.

FLOWERS

Seeing blooming flowers on the way to the wedding site augurs a fertile marriage with many children. Be sure not to pick the flowers, however: This could alter your luck.

GREEN GRASS

Green grass at a wedding site, especially in early spring-time, is a sign of future success in business.

HAIRPINS

Hairpins bring good luck. Use eight of them on your wedding hairstyle (or a multiple of eight) and your good fortune will be multiplied.

HORSESHOE

A horseshoe is an age-old symbol of good luck. Have your flower girl or ring bearer carry a small horseshoe charm as they walk up the aisle, or wear a necklace with a horseshoe pendant down the aisle. Remember that a horseshoe is most powerful when its ends are pointing up.

IVY

Climbing ivy on a building or house signifies prosperity. Keep your eye out for some as you travel to and from your wedding ceremony.

KEYS

One key alone is not much of an omen, but three keys together can unlock the doors to love, health, and wealth. The night before the wedding, give your fiancé three small keys, and have him carry them in his breast pocket, close to his heart, on the wedding day.

MIRROR

A mirror reflects and intensifies light. When looked into by two lovers, it can also intensify the love they feel for each other. Find a room with a mirror at your reception site, and stand for a few minutes in it with your mate on your wedding day.

MISTLETOE

Mistletoe is best known as a prelude to a kiss at the holidays. But when used at a wedding, it also foretells a blessing of long life and happiness to come after a promise of marriage.

NECKTIE

A properly tied tie foretells romantic success, especially when tied by someone who has already made a successful marriage. Choose a relative whose marriage is particularly strong and ask that person to tie your mate's tie for him on the wedding day.

ORANGES

If you use oranges (with their stems and leaves attached) as centerpieces for your wedding table, you will have good health all your life. And if your mate buys the oranges himself, and if you eat one, the two of you will soon come into some money.

PLAYING CARDS

The ace of hearts and the ace of diamonds are the most auspicious cards—held together, they augur luck in both love and money. Give them to the best man to slip into his pocket during the ceremony.

RAILROAD TRACKS

Crossing railroad tracks on the way to or from a wedding ceremony augurs good luck. Drive out of your way to cross them if you must, but the greatest fortune will come if you come upon the tracks inadvertently.

SCISSORS

Greek legend has it that scissors "cut the evil eye" and protect from harm. On your wedding day, snip a stem from your bouquet and give it to a person you feel needs sheltering.

UMBRELLAS

Just as umbrellas provide literal protection from rain, they offer protection from harm when used at a wedding. If the wedding day is rainy, you're in luck. If the day is sunny, pass out parasols to your female guests and bring protection to all the wedding attendees.

WRISTWATCHES

Catching sight of a particularly distinctive wristwatch on the arm of a relative during any wedding event (especially the rehearsal dinner) means that another close relative will soon be married.

THE BIG DAY

In medieval weddings, the bride stood to the left of her groom during the ceremony. This allowed the groom to have his sword arm free to fight off other suitors who wished to take the bride for their own. While you likely will not need your groom to draw his sword on your wedding day, there are many other details about the big day to pay attention to: They hold meaning for your future lives together. . . .

LOCATION

Close to home or far away, the city or the country, his hometown or yours—where you choose to have your wedding can hold the key to future happiness.

IF YOUR WEDDING TAKES PLACE . . .
IN THE GROOM'S HOMETOWN:

A wedding in the groom's hometown may mean the two of you will be faced with an important decision during the first year of marriage. Consult each other, and follow your instincts, though they may seem impractical.

IN THE BRIDE'S HOMETOWN:

If observed carefully, your investments will pay off.

IN THE PLACE WHERE YOU LIVE:

As a couple, you and your mate have a welcoming spirit about you and are constantly making new friends. You are easy to spend time with, and people enjoy your company.

AT A DESTINATION SITE:

You have many latent talents. Consider taking time off from work to explore what you really love. It is likely that this will lead you in a positive new direction.

WEDDING VENUE

The venue you select for your wedding carries with it meaning. Which one fits you best?

IF YOU GET MARRIED . . .
IN A CHURCH:

You prefer to stay close to home, but you are not a loner—you love the company of friends and you can be quite social. You are an excellent conversationalist and people always hope to have you as a guest at their parties.

AT HOME (YOURS OR ANOTHER'S):

You are too modest. Toot your own horn and you will be surprised at the opportunities and accolades that fall in your path.

OUTDOORS:

You have an artistic, poetic nature about you. You are patient and thoughtful and would make a very good teacher.

ON A BEACH:

You can expect very good news during the winter following your wedding.

IN A BALLROOM:

An unexpected yet very promising career opportunity lies in your future. You are more comfortable following than leading, and this will give you the chance to do so and still shine.

IN A HOTEL:

You are easily put off and as such usually follow the path of least resistance. Remember to step outside your comfort zone now and again—you will be surprised at how much you can accomplish.

AT A MUSEUM:

You have an ability to make people feel very special.
Because of it, people will always be drawn to you, and they
feel truly honored in your presence.

ATTENDANTS

Who will stand up by your side as you say "I do"? The attendants you have for your wedding are a reflection of your true self.

IF YOU HAVE . . .
NO ATTENDANTS:

You have a difficult time with authority, but fortunately you also have a good business sense. The only person you work for should be yourself.

1-2 ATTENDANTS:

You are strong-willed and ruled by logic and reason rather than emotions. You will be very successful, but do not forget to tap into your softer side every now and again.

3-5 ATTENDANTS:

You are ambitious and have the ability to persevere through difficult times. You will continue to strive to do your best, and it will pay off in spades.

6 OR MORE ATTENDANTS:

You are energetic and enthusiastic, and always up for an adventure. You have a star quality about you that draws people to you. You are very loyal to your friends, and usually receive the same in return.

IF YOUR ATTENDANTS ARE ALL FAMILY MEMBERS:

You tend not to show your true feelings unless they are happy ones. Work on opening up and saying what you mean. You will reap the benefits.

TIME OF DAY

It is most fortuitous if you and your beloved exchange vows and rings as the minute hand of the clock is pointing upwards. So depending on how long your ceremony will be, try and time it so the vows take place near the top of an hour.

IF YOU GET MARRIED BETWEEN . . .
9 A.M. AND 12 NOON:

The wedding will go off without a hitch. And that one family member you were worried might make a scene will remain calm throughout it all.

12 NOON AND 4 P.M.:

Your first child will be a girl.

4 P.M. AND 8 P.M.:

An old friend will make it to the ceremony in just the nick of time—and will have good news for you.

DOWN THE AISLE

Here comes the bride! You will be stunning no matter how you come down the aisle, but read on to see what is in store for your choice.

IF YOU AND YOUR FIANCÉ
WALK TOGETHER:

In the latter part of your lives together, you and your husband will travel a great deal.

IF YOU WALK WITH YOUR FATHER:

You have a persuasive way about you. Tap into it when you need to get things from others.

IF YOU WALK WITH BOTH PARENTS:

The good character of others is very important to you. You have equally high expectations of yourself, and are known for your dignity, honesty, and wisdom.

IF YOU WALK WITH ANOTHER RELATIVE:

You are always up for a challenge. Your powers of motivation are quite strong. Consider leading a team or starting a business—those under you will be all too happy to do as you advise.

IF YOU WALK BY YOURSELF:

Adversity does not discourage you. Your vast powers of concentration will get you through rough times.

IF YOU MEET YOUR FIANCÉ HALFWAY DOWN THE AISLE:

You are a lifelong learner. Continue to take classes, read, and improve yourself throughout your life. You will take great joy in spreading that knowledge to others.

GREAT PLATES

Food holds great meaning. It can bring luck and happiness, usher in fertility, and offer protection from harm. Choose your wedding food according to the portent that each brings and you will be lucky indeed....

WEDDING FOOD

Serve the following foods at your wedding reception for greatest fortune. And don't forget wedding favors: In earlier days, wedding guests took home leftover food from the wedding in order to bring abundance upon themselves. Today, edible wedding favors (small boxes of chocolates, a takeaway bottle of wine for each guest) have the same effect. Favors in red packaging will bring added benefit: future happiness for your guests.

AVOCADO

You will have healthy and beautiful children.

BACON

Serve bacon at your wedding, and wealth is just around the corner.

BEEF

Serve beef cooked medium, and you and your husband will reap success in business.

CARROTS

Carrots augur prosperity when cut into round slices, and good health when cut into sticks. Serve them both ways for the greatest benefit!

CHAMPAGNE

Raise a glass of champagne in a toast and you ensure that your vivacity on the wedding day will not fade. If you do not imbibe, sparkling water or other fizzy beverages can bring the same effect.

CHEESE

Cheese, especially aged cheese, is a harbinger of lasting romance. Serve it at your wedding in passed hors d'oeuvres or on an appetizer buffet.

CHERRIES

Cherries, both raw and cooked, point to successful love and an easy, happy marriage.

CHICKEN

Success in work affairs is augured for you. For greatest benefit, choose roast chicken instead of stewed, poached, or boiled.

CHOCOLATE

Chocolate at your wedding means you and your husband
will always be able to provide for your family.

CRAB

Crab brings good luck, especially when consumed in the
winter months.

DATES

Dates usher in fertility—if you want three or more children,
serve them at your wedding.

EGGS

Eggs bring good fortune of all kinds.

FRUIT

Fruit at a wedding, especially very ripe fruit, is a sign of good health for years to come.

GARLIC

Include garlic in wedding dishes, and you and your loved ones will receive protection from harm.

GRAPEFRUIT

Grapefruit chases away bitterness and evil.

HONEY

Honey forecasts health, wealth, and a sweet life.

ICE CREAM

Ice cream is particularly fortuitous: Eaten at a wedding, it will bring abundance, happiness, and many children.

LETTUCE

Serving green lettuce at a wedding forecasts a period of great enjoyment after a minor embarrassment has been resolved.

LOBSTER

Serve lobster at your wedding dinner and you will have a fulfilled and joyful life. But be careful to serve the lobster whole rather than in pieces—a whole lobster symbolizes completeness in your relationship.

MINT

Mint is a noted aphrodisiac—for you and your new husband, as well as your wedding guests!

OLIVES

Serve olives at your wedding, and decorate tables with the leaves and branches of the olive tree, and your marriage will be a peaceful one.

OMELETTES

Omelettes are harbingers of fertility. Eat them on your honeymoon, and leave the rest up to fate!

PANCAKES

Pancakes will draw new friends to you.

PASTA

Pasta at a wedding reception (especially long, thin noodles) means longevity for you and your mate.

PINEAPPLE

Eat pineapple at your wedding, and you and your husband will be well regarded in your social circles.

RED WINE

Red wine stands for the love shared between close friends. Serve it at your wedding and ensure a life full of happy hours whiled away with companions.

ROSEMARY

You and your husband always will be faithful to each other, and will beget many children, if you partake of rosemary at your wedding.

SALT

Salt brings forth wealth. It is especially auspicious when paired with bread.

TOMATOES

Tomatoes at your wedding, especially in cooked dishes, mean you will travel far and wide during your marriage.

WALNUTS

Walnuts forecast prolific joy in your life together. If you serve them unshelled, and have guests open them with nutcrackers, joy will be theirs as well.

WHEAT

Wheat and grain are signs of fertility and good fortune. Serve bread at your wedding table and good luck and children are sure to follow.

RECIPES FOR LOVE

After you have tied the knot, bring in more good fortune by preparing these recipes.

SPICY VEGETABLE-GINGER NOODLES

This dish brings together carrots for prosperity, noodles for long life, garlic for protection, honey for happiness, and finally, mint as an aphrodisiac. What more could a new couple need?

1 tablespoon vegetable oil

4 tablespoons grated fresh ginger

3 teaspoons minced garlic

2 carrots, peeled and diced

1 zucchini, diced

3 green onions, diced

1 teaspoon sesame oil

1 cup water

1/4 cup oyster sauce

1 cup coconut milk (unsweetened)

1 tablespoon honey

1 tablespoon soy sauce

1 1/2 teaspoons red curry paste

1 8-ounce package soba noodles

Salt

Pepper

1/2 cup finely chopped peanuts

1/2 cup finely chopped mint leaves

In large skillet heat vegetable oil over high heat. Add the ginger and garlic and sauté until fragrant, about 30 seconds. Add the carrots, zucchini, half of the green onions, and all of the sesame oil. Sauté until vegetables are crisp-tender. Transfer the vegetables to a bowl using a slotted spoon.

Reduce the heat to medium. Add the water, oyster sauce, coconut milk, honey, soy sauce, and curry paste to the same skillet. Stir until smooth. Simmer until sauce is reduced to 1¼ cups, about 7 minutes. Add the sautéed vegetables and the remaining onions.

Meanwhile, cook the soba noodles according to package directions. Drain and transfer to a large bowl. Add the vegetables and toss to coat. Season with salt and pepper to taste. Garnish with the peanuts and mint, and serve.

Serves 2, with leftovers

CRAB SALAD WITH AVOCADO AND GRAPEFRUIT

Crab for good luck, avocado for healthy offspring, salt for prosperity, and grapefruit to keep the family happy and safe from harm. This is a combination the fates approve of.

1 large grapefruit

2 teaspoons finely chopped shallots

1 tablespoon lemon juice

1/4 teaspoon kosher salt

2 tablespoons extra-virgin olive oil

1 ripe avocado

6 ounces cooked crabmeat

2 cups baby arugula

Coarse sea salt

Cut the peel and the white pith from the grapefruit. Cut segments free from membranes and drain segments on paper towels. Squeeze the remaining membranes over a bowl to reserve about 1 tablespoon of the juice.

In a small bowl, combine the shallots, lemon juice, reserved grapefruit juice, and kosher salt and let stand at room temperature 30 minutes. Whisk in the olive oil.

Halve the avocado lengthwise (save one half for another use). Discard the pit, halve the remaining avocado half lengthwise, and peel, then cut crosswise into 1/4-inch-thick slices.

Divide the avocado and crabmeat between two salad plates and arrange the grapefruit around them. Top with the arugula and drizzle with dressing. Sprinkle with sea salt to taste and serve immediately.

Serves 2

HONEYMOONERS

Now that the wedding is over, you and your new husband can breathe a sigh of relief, and indulge in some much-needed rest. But the fates are still working for you. And how you choose to spend your post-wedding time can bring you even more good fortune. . . .

THE HONEYMOON

What is your honeymoon plan? Rest, relax, and let more luck come your way with one of these choices.

CLOSE TO HOME

If you choose a honeymoon destination within one day's driving distance of where you live, your future home will be a gathering place for friends and family, and you and your mate will live to a very old age together in great comfort.

NEAR WATER

If you take your honeymoon near a large body of water, you will receive a very pleasant surprise in the mail during your second year of marriage.

CRUISING

If you go on a cruise to celebrate your honeymoon, expect a desire to beautify your surroundings once you return home.

TRAIN TRAVEL

If your honeymoon includes travel by train, an unexpected surge of daring will come upon you, whether it is on the honeymoon itself or afterwards. Embrace this new side of yourself and you and your husband will both be pleased.

BICYCLING

A bicycle adventure during your honeymoon could mean a flash of insight is coming your way. If you have been trying to solve a particular problem, the answer may be just around the corner.

HISTORICAL SITES

If your honeymoon includes a tour of ancient sites or ruins, you will become reacquainted with a long-lost friend soon after you return home.

SKIING

Go skiing on your honeymoon and either you or your husband will be asked to be the leader of a group or organization once you return home.

SCUBA DIVING

Scuba diving on the honeymoon may mean that the two of you will become restless with one part of your current life. After the honeymoon, seek out change.

HORSEBACK RIDING

Saddle up during your honeymoon and you will meet some very interesting new people. Keep in touch with them after the honeymoon—they have much to offer.

YOUR NAME

After the wedding, will you keep your own last name, take that of your husband, or go a different route altogether? Your choice shows a great deal about you.

IF YOU TAKE YOUR HUSBAND'S NAME:

You are very adaptable and take to change easily. You are kind, gentle, and honest. You don't share your secrets easily, but once you take friends into your confidence you trust in them completely. You are an excellent listener and have a very empathetic nature.

IF YOU KEEP YOUR OWN NAME:

You know your own mind. Though you may ask others for advice, the counsel you follow is most often your own. You enjoy conversation but prefer it to be on an intellectual level. Your family is of utmost importance to you.

IF YOU CREATE A NEW NAME FOR THE TWO OF YOU, OR HYPHENATE YOUR NAMES:

You are a planner at heart. Your actions are well considered and deliberate, and you can be stubborn when you feel you are right. You have a tendency to analyze people and situations around you, which will serve you well as long as you don't overdo it.

YOUR NEW HOME

After the honeymoon, you and your husband will settle into a new life in your home together. As per tradition (and for good luck), your mate can carry you over the threshold of your dwelling the first time you enter it together as husband and wife. But you can do much more than that to ensure that good fortune continues to follow you.

BREAD

A freshly baked loaf of bread presented as a housewarming gift foretells a life in which you will always have enough to eat.

BROOM

If you are moving together into a new home, do not bring an already-used broom into your new dwelling—and if you must bring it, pass it through the window, not the door. Ideally, friends or family should bring you a new broom, which will sweep away any old evil from the house. When you move away from the house, leave the broom—it will bring the new owners the same luck you have had. By the same token, finding an old broom in your new home when you move in is a very auspicious omen.

CANDLE

Light candles around your home on your first evening there together, and you will be blessed with a marriage of clarity and understanding.

COINS

Place three coins under your doormat or just inside your front door, and you will usher in prosperity and good fortune for the first year of your marriage.

HONEY

Share a spoonful of honey with your mate on your first few days as husband and wife, and your life together will always be sweet.

KNIFE

Buy a new set of knives for your kitchen and powerful good spirits will watch over you and protect you from any harm. If you receive the knives as a wedding or housewarming present, be sure to send the gift-giver a penny in return, for it is bad luck to accept a knife without payment of some kind.

OLIVE OIL

Use olive oil in some capacity on your first day in your home together. It will usher in health, light, and fidelity to the marriage.

OWL

An owl figurine placed near a door or window will ward off evil and bring good luck.

PLANT

A young, thriving plant (or a transplanted clipping from an established plant) will provide longevity to your union. Watch over the plant carefully and this portent will hold even more true.

SALT

A package of salt brought into a new dwelling can ensure that your life together will always be interesting, and few troubles will come your way. You can also place a pinch of salt at the threshold of each door and window to attract good luck.

WINE

Share a bottle of wine with your husband on your first evening together in your home, and your home will bring you happiness and joy for as long as you live in it.

WOOD

Something made of wood (a bowl, a chair, a frame, or so on) that is brought into the home of a newlywed couple augurs stability, harmony, and peace for the marriage.

Do all these things, and you and your mate will live and love together in great happiness and harmony for the rest of your days.

WEDDING BLESSINGS
FROM AROUND THE WORLD

APACHE WEDDING BLESSING

Now you will feel no rain,
for each of you will be shelter for the other.

Now you will feel no cold,
for each of you will be warmth to the other.

Now there is no more loneliness.

Now you are two persons,
but there is only one life before you.

Go now to your dwelling place,
to enter into the days of your togetherness.

And may your days be good and long upon the earth.

AZTEC WEDDING BLESSING

I know not whether thou has been absent:

I lie down with thee, I rise up with thee,

In my dreams thou art with me.

If my eardrops tremble in my ears,

I know it is thou moving within my heart.

CHINESE WEDDING BLESSING

I want to be your friend

For ever and ever without break or decay.

When the hills are all flat

And the rivers are all dry,

When it lightens and thunders in winter,

When it rains and snows in summer,

When Heaven and Earth mingle

Not 'til then will I part from you.

ENGLISH WEDDING BLESSING

May your joys be as bright as the morning,

your years of happiness

as numerous as the stars in the heavens,

and your troubles but shadows

that fade in the sunlight of love.

GERMAN WEDDING BLESSING

I am yours. You are mine.

Of this we are certain.

You are lodged in my heart, the small key is lost.

You must stay there forever.

HINDU WEDDING BLESSING

May the nights be honey-sweet for us.

May the mornings be honey-sweet for us.

May the plants be honey-sweet for us.

May the earth be honey-sweet for us.

INUIT WEDDING BLESSING

You are my husband/wife.

My feet shall run because of you.

My feet dance because of you.

My eyes see because of you.

My mind thinks because of you.

And I shall love because of you.

IRISH WEDDING BLESSING

May the road rise to meet you,

May the wind be always at your back,

May the sun shine warm upon your face,

May the rain fall soft upon your fields,

And, until we meet again,

May God hold you in the hollow of his hand.

JEWISH WEDDING BLESSING

From every human being there rises a light that reaches straight to heaven, and when two souls that are designed to be together find each other, their streams of light flow together and a single, brighter light goes forth from their united being.

NAVAJO WEDDING BLESSING

Now you have lit a fire and that fire should not go out.

The two of you now have a fire that represents love,

understanding, and a philosophy of life.

It will give you heat, food, warmth, and happiness.

The new fire represents a new beginning—

a new life and a new family.

The fire is to be kept burning; you are meant
to stay together.

You have lit this fire for life, until only old age
separates you.

PERSIAN WEDDING BLESSING

This is love: to fly toward a secret sky,
to cause a hundred veils to fall each moment.

First to let go of life.

Finally, to take a step without feet.

SCOTTISH WEDDING BLESSING

If there is righteousness in the heart
there will be beauty in the character,

If there is beauty in the character
there will be harmony in the home.

If there is harmony in the home,
there will be order in the nation.

If there is order in the nation,
there will be peace in the world.

So let it be.

WELSH WEDDING BLESSING

Wishing you

A house full of sunshine,

Hearts full of cheer,

Love that grows deeper

each day of the year.

SUFI WEDDING BLESSING

Is love pleasure, is love merriment?

No, love is longing constantly;

Love is persevering unweariedly;

Love is hoping patiently;

Love is willing surrender;

Love is regarding constantly the pleasure
and displeasure of the beloved,

For love is resignation to the will
of the possessor of one's heart;

It is love that teaches us: Thou, not I.

WEDDING ANNIVERSARIES

	TRADITIONAL	MODERN	FLOWER GIFTS
1	Paper	Clocks	Carnation
2	Cotton	China	Lily of the Valley
3	Leather	Crystal	Sunflower
4	Fruit or Flowers	Appliances	Hydrangea
5	Wood	Silverware	Daisy
6	Sugar or Iron	Wood	Calla
7	Wool or Copper	Desk Sets	Freesia
8	Bronze or Pottery	Linens or Lace	Lilac
9	Pottery or Willow	Leather	Bird-of-Paradise
10	Tin or Aluminum	Diamond Jewelry	Daffodil
11	Steel	Jewelry	Tulip
12	Silk or Linen	Pearls	Peony
13	Lace	Textiles or Furs	Chrysanthemum
14	Ivory	Gold Jewelry	Dahlia
15	Crystal	Watches	Rose
16		Silver Holloware	
17		Furniture	

	TRADITIONAL	MODERN	FLOWER GIFTS
18		Porcelain	
19		Bronze	
20	China	Platinum	Aster
21		Brass or Nickel	
22		Copper	
23		Silver Plate	
24		Musical Instruments	
25	Silver	Silver	Iris
28			Orchid
30	Pearl	Diamond	Lily
35	Coral	Jade	
40	Ruby	Ruby	Gladiolus
45	Sapphire	Sapphire	
50	Gold	Gold	Yellow Rose or Violet
55	Emerald	Emerald	
60	Diamond	Diamond	
70	Platinum	Platinum	

Text copyright © 2009 by Chronicle Books LLC.
Text by K. C. Jones.
Illustrations copyright © 2009 A. J. Garcés.

Library of Congress Cataloging-in-Publication Data available.
ISBN 978-0-8118-7014-6

Manufactured in China.
Design by Catherine Grishaver.
Illustrations by A. J. Garcés.

Typeset in Neutra and Memphis.

Chronicle Books endeavors to use environmentally responsible
paper in its gift and stationery products.

10 9 8 7 6 5 4 3 2 1

Chronicle Books LLC
680 Second Street
San Francisco, CA 94107
www.chroniclebooks.com